PTERANODON

THE FLYING REPTILE

by

Elizabeth J. Sandell

DINOSAUR DISCOVERY ERA

Bancroft-Sage Publishing

601 Elkcam Circle, Suite C-7, Box 355, Marco, FL 33969

Exclusive distributor

ENCYCLOPAEDIA BRITANNICA EDUCATIONAL CORPORATION

TRAINING & DEVELOPMENT

310 South Michigan Avenue Chicago, IL 60604

LIBRARY OF CONGRESS CATALOGING IN PUBLICATION DATA

Sandell, Elizabeth J.
   Pteranodon: the flying reptile.

   (Dinosaur discovery era)
   SUMMARY: Discusses what is presently believed about the flying reptiles of the dinosaur age known as pteranodon.
   1. Pteranodon--Juvenile literature. (1. Pteranodon. 2. Prehistoric animals) I. Oelerich, Marjorie L. II. Schroeder, Howard. III. Vista III Design. IV. Title. V. Series.
   QE862.P7S27   1988   567.9'7   88-953
   ISBN 0-944280-05-6 (lib. bdg.)
   ISBN 0-944280-11-0 (pbk bdg.)

International Standard Book Number:	Library of Congress Catalog Card Number:
Library Binding 0-944280-05-6	88-953
Paperback Binding 0-944280-11-0	

SPECIAL THANKS FOR THEIR HELP AND COOPERATION TO:
S. Christopher Bennett, Department of Systematics and Ecology, and Museum of Natural History, Univ. of Kansas, Lawrence, Kansas
and
Mary R. Carman, Paleontology Collection Manager
Field Museum of Natural History, Chicago, Illinois

PTERANODON

THE FLYING REPTILE

AUTHOR
Elizabeth J. Sandell

dedicated with appreciation to Gretchen Etzell

EDITED BY
Marjorie L. Oelerich, Ph.D.
Professor of Early Childhood and Elementary Education
Mankato State University

Howard Schroeder, Ph.D.
Professor of Reading and Language Arts
Dept. of Curriculum and Instruction
Mankato State University
Mankato, MN

ILLUSTRATED BY
Vista III Design

BANCROFT-SAGE PUBLISHING
112 Marshall St., Box 1968, Mankato, MN 56001-1968 U.S.A.

INTRODUCTION:
MATTHEW GOES ON A "DIG"

Dr. Sanford came to visit Matthew's class at school. Mr. Finley, the teacher, told the class that Dr. Sanford was a paleontologist. Paleontologists are special scientists who study fossils.

Scientists like Dr. Sanford look at fossils for clues about what life was like thousands of years ago.

"Fossils give us information about animals which lived on the earth long ago," said Dr. Sanford. "Some of these animals are known as dinosaurs, pterosaurs, or other group names. Everything we know about all these animals comes from the fossils that scientists find."

"When I grow up, I want to be a paleontologist. Then I will be able to study fossils like you do," Matthew said to Dr. Sanford. "I want to learn about dinosaurs, pterosaurs, and other animals which lived long ago! I want to learn more about what these animals looked like, how they lived, and what they ate."

"Matthew, if you would like to learn more about fossils now," Dr. Sanford said, "you could take a Saturday class at our Museum of Natural History."

5

After Dr. Sanford said good-bye and Matthew returned home from school, he asked his parents to call the museum office. The museum people said there was a class called "Dinosaur Dig for a Day." It was a one-day "dig" for students to go with scientists on a "dig" to look for fossils.

That sounded like a good idea to Matthew. So that weekend he went to the Saturday class.

A bus took the group of students from the museum to the field. Dr. Sanford went with them. While they rode the bus, she told about finding and studying fossils.

"More fossils from dinosaurs and other animals are found every year. When paleontologists find fossil bones and teeth, they figure out the kind of animal from which the fossils came," Dr. Sanford explained. "Then the scientists put the fossils together into skeletons."

At the "dig," the students worked in groups of two or three. The place for each group to dig was outlined with ropes tied to stakes in the ground. Students used chisels and hammers to tap away the rock. They also used their fingers to move small bits of dirt. They picked up loose pieces of rock and dirt — just a little at a time. Sometimes the students used a small brush to sweep away the dust.

While Matthew's group looked for fossils in the dirt, Dr. Sanford told them about pterosaurs, which were flying reptiles. She had a great deal to tell about one kind of pterosaurs, which was called *Pteranodon*.

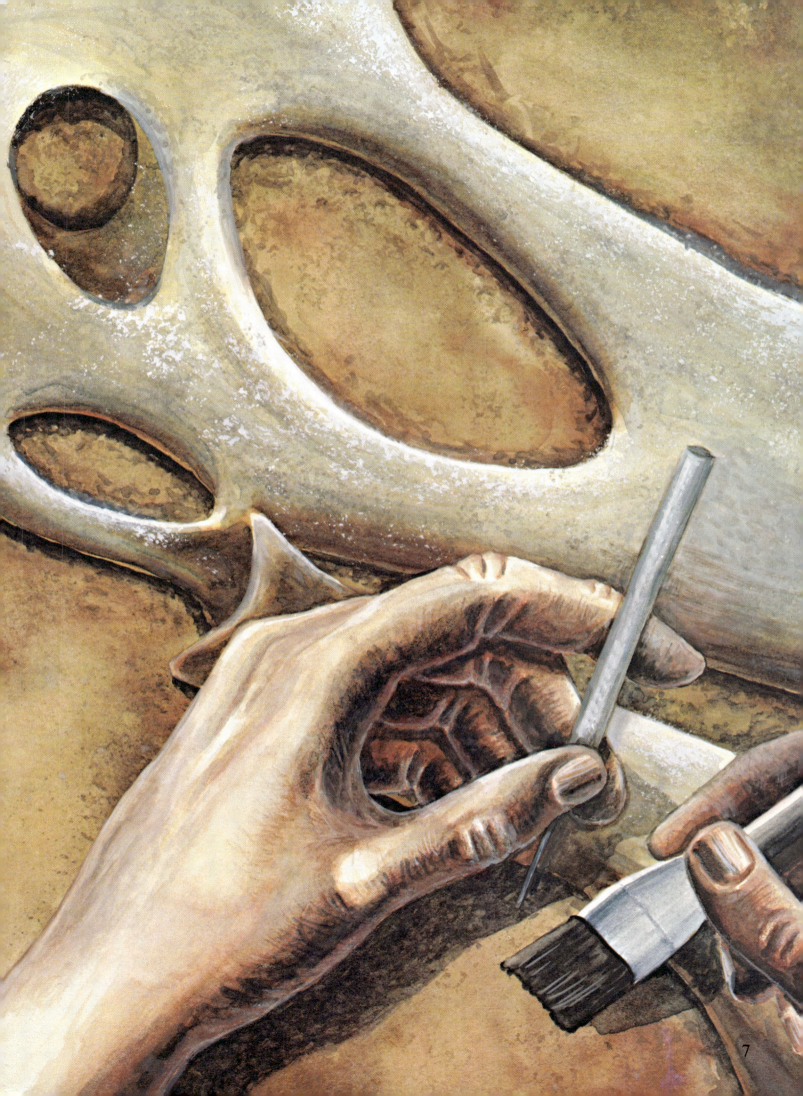

CHAPTER 1:
PTERANODON WAS
A FLYING REPTILE

Pteranodon (ter an´ uh don) was not a dinosaur. It was a flying reptile.

Pteranodon means "winged and toothless," because these animals had wings but no teeth. The name was made from the Greek words **pteron** for wing, and **anodontos,** which means "toothless."

Pteranodon's wings did not have feathers. Some paleontologists (pa´ le on tol´ uh jists) believe that it had some kind of fur or hair to cover the skin, which was like leather.

APPEARANCE OF PTERANODON

The body of *Pteranodon* was the size of a large turkey. It weighed 15 to 33 pounds (6.75 to 15 kg).

There was a big flat plate of bone at the back of the head of some *Pteranodons*. This was called a crest. Some scientists believe that only the males had a crest. This crest may have helped the animal make turns when it was in the air.

9

WINGS AND FEET

The wings of *Pteranodon* could spread 15 to 25 feet (4.6 to 8 m) wide. This would be as wide as five or six children, standing side by side, with their arms spread out.

There were three small fingers with claws at the joint in each wing. In addition, there was a longer fourth finger, which had four long bones. The wings were stretched from the side of the body to the tip of this fourth finger.

The wings were made of thin, leathery skin. The skin was stretched across the bones, like a bat's wings.

Two small feet were attached to thin legs. Scientists do not know for sure how *Pteranodon* used these feet. Some experts think that maybe *Pteranodon* could crawl, like a bat. Other paleontologists believe that it could run on its legs to get enough speed to start flying.

The bones were hollow, like the bones of birds. This made the *Pteranodon* weigh less, so it could fly higher and longer.

FLYING OR GLIDING

"*Pteranodon* probably did not have very strong wing muscles," said S. Christopher Bennett. Bennett is a paleontologist at the University of Kansas. He has reported about how this animal would glide through the air.

"Its wings may have been used more for gliding, like flying a kite," Bennett said. "This flying reptile would use its muscles to flap these wings to reach the high, fast winds. Then it could coast away over the seas."

14

Pteranodon might have glided along at 12 to 30 miles (20 to 50 km) each hour. Its large head helped it change directions easily.

Out to sea, *Pteranodon* looked down to find food. With large eyes, it could see very small fish in the water. Scientists believe it would fly low over the water and dive down. Its long, sharp beak could stab the fish near the top of the water.

CHAPTER 2: LIFE OF PTERANODON

Pteranodon lived thousands of years ago. When *Pteranodon* lived, the land may have been joined like the map below.

A warm, shallow sea covered the land from the Gulf of Mexico to the Arctic Ocean. This sea covered some parts of the United States now called Texas, Kansas, North Dakota, and South Dakota.

Skeletons of *Pteranodon* have been found in Kansas and South Dakota (USA), where the bottom of the seas turned into rock. Fossil bones of the fish which *Pteranodon* hunted for food have also been found.

Other pterosaurs (ter´ uh sorz´) like *Pteranodon* have been found in Delaware (USA); England and Germany (Europe); Brazil (South America); and Australia.

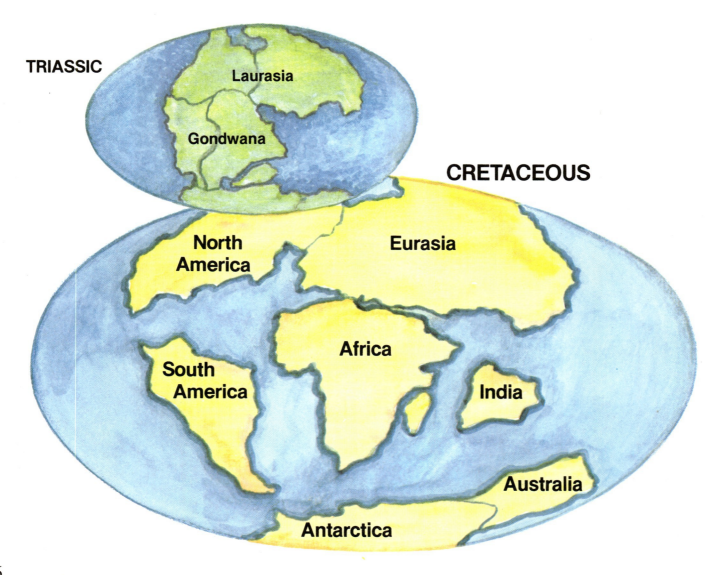

Pteranodon might have built nests on empty islands away from its enemies. The females laid eggs in the nests. Young *Pteranodon* probably could not fly until their wings grew long. The parents brought food to them.

Fossil fish bones have been found near *Pteranodon* fossils. This suggests that this flying reptile ate fish. Since fossils of other animals have not been found near *Pteranodon* fossils, scientists believe that it did not eat other animals.

DANGERS ON THE LAND AND IN THE SEAS

There were dangers on the land. Dinosaurs and other large animals might attack *Pteranodon*. They might tear the skin of the wings of *Pteranodon*. When this happened, it would have to stay on the ground. Then meat-eating animals could catch it.

There were also dangers in the seas. If *Pteranodon* flew too low, a *Tylosaurus* (ti´ lo sor´ uhs) or an *Elasmosaurus* (i laz´ muh sor´ uhs) might jump out of the water and grab it. The jagged teeth of these meat-eaters would rip the wings and break the bones of *Pteranodon*. If its enemies pulled *Pteranodon* into the water, it would drown.

CHAPTER 3:
THE LARGEST FLYING REPTILE

Scientists used to think that *Pteranodon* was the largest flying reptile because its wings were so long. However, fossils of another animal have been found with wings even longer.

In 1971, Douglas Lawson found a bone from another flying reptile at Big Bend National Park, in Texas (USA). The wings of this animal were at least 35 to 40 feet (11 to 12 m) wide.

Lawson considered it to be like *Pteranodon.* He included it in a group of animals called pterosaur. This particular animal he named Quetzalcoatlus (ket sal´ ko a´ tel uhs).

Lawson found more bones, in 1972 and in 1974, of more pterosaurs. Other bones from Quetzalcoatlus were found in Oregon, Wyoming, and New Jersey (USA). The scientists compared these bones with other pterosaur bones. They think that Quetzalcoatlus might even have had wings that were up to 51 feet (16 m) wide. That is wider than the wings of some airplanes.

Scientists compare Quetzalcoatlus to the largest living birds, such as condors and vultures. Like these birds, Quetzalcoatlus, with its three-foot (.9 m) long toothless beak, may have eaten dead animals on the ground.

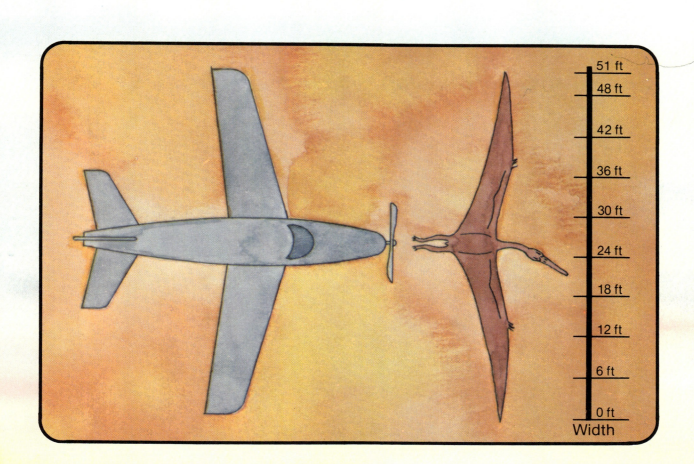

51 ft
48 ft
42 ft
36 ft
30 ft
24 ft
18 ft
12 ft
6 ft
0 ft
Width

CHAPTER 4:
WHEN THEY DISAPPEARED

Pteranodon, Quetzalcoatlus, and the other pterosaurs disappeared thousands of years ago. This was about the same time that the dinosaurs disappeared.

Scientists have many different ideas about why all these animals died. Somehow, the weather changed, and the air became colder.

Scientists are not sure how this change in the weather happened. Maybe a huge rock, over six miles (10 km) across, came from space and hit the earth. Dust from this crash may have blocked out the sunlight, so that the air cooled off.

A star might have exploded in space and caused rays of energy to kill these animals.

Maybe there was a disease that killed dinosaurs and other animals.

Whatever happened, there were no more dinosaurs and no more pterosaurs.

When the animals died, their bodies were covered with sand and mud. Some bones turned into fossils, which paleontologists now find in fields and rocks.

CONCLUSION: AFTER THE "DIG"

"This was great!" Matthew told his parents when they met him at the bus to take him home. "On this dig, I watched the museum workers who help discover fossils.

"When I grow up," Matthew said, "I could be a paleontologist to study fossil plants and animals. Or I could be a geologist to know about the kinds of rocks that have fossils. Or I could be an

artist to draw pictures to show how the fossils were found.

"I could be one of the workers to help dig the fossils," continued Matthew. "Maybe I could be a photographer to take pictures of the place where the fossils are found. Or I could be another worker to pack the fossils and send them back to the museum. There are many things to do in learning about dinosaurs and pterosaurs!"

29

MUSEUMS

Exhibits of Pteranodon may be seen at the following museums:

American Museum of Natural History, New York, NY.

Carnegie Museum, Pittsburgh, PA.

Los Angeles County Museum of Natural History, Los Angeles, CA.

Museum of Comparative Zoology, Boston, MA.

National Museum of Natural History, Smithsonian Institution, Washington, DC.

Natural History Museum, University of Kansas, Lawrence, KS.

Peabody Museum of Natural History, Yale University, New Haven, CT.

Sternberg Memorial Museum, Hays, KS.

GLOSSARY

DIG (dig) is a special trip to fields and rocks in order to dig for fossils.

DINOSAUR (di´ nuh sor´) means "terrible lizard." The Greek word **deinos** means "terrible," and the word **sauros** means "lizard."

ELASMOSAURUS (i laz´ muh sor´ uhs) was a long-necked plesiosaur that was about 43 feet (13 m) long and moved with paddle-like flippers. The word is from the Greek **elasmos** which means "thin plate" and **sauros** which means "lizard."

FOSSILS (fos´ uhlz) are the remains of plants and animals that lived many years ago. The Latin word **fossilis** means "something dug up."

GEOLOGIST (je ol´ uh jist) is a person who studies rocks and fossils and how the layers of the rocks were made.

MUSEUM (myoo ze´ uhm) is a place for keeping and exhibiting works of nature and art, scientific objects, and other items.

PALEONTOLOGIST (pa´ le on tol´ uh jist) is a person who studies fossils to learn about plants and animals from thousands of years ago. The Greek word **palaios** means "ancient," **onta** means "living things," and **logos** means "talking about."

PTERANODON (ter an´ uh don) was a large flying reptile that did not have teeth. The word is from the Greek **pteron** which means "wing" and **anodontos** which means "toothless."

PTEROSAURS (ter´ uh sorz´) were flying reptiles. They no longer exist.

QUETZALCOATLUS (ket sal´ ko a´ tel uhs) was a giant pterosaur. It was the largest known flying creature.

REPTILES (rep´ tilz) are cold-blooded, egg-laying animals, such as snakes, alligators, and lizards. The legs grow out of the sides of the body, causing the reptile to crawl instead of walk. The Latin word **reptilis** means "creeping."

SCIENTIST (si´ uhn tist) is a person who studies objects or events.

SKELETON (skel´ uh tuhn) is the framework of bones of a body.

THOUSAND (thou´ zuhnd) is ten times one hundred. It is shown as 1,000.

TYLOSAURUS (ti´ lo sor´ uhs) was a large, meat-eating lizard that lived in the sea. It was 20 to 40 feet (6 to 12 m) long, with a slim body. It had sharp teeth and flipper-like legs. The word is from the Greek **tylos** which means "knot" and the word **sauros** which means "lizard."

TIME LINE

PERIOD

CHARACTERISTIC ANIMAL LIFE

AGE OF THE DINOSAURS

CRETACEOUS
65 MILLION YEARS TO
135 MILLION YEARS AGO

JURASSIC
136 MILLION YEARS TO
192 MILLION YEARS AGO

TRIASSIC
193 MILLION YEARS TO
224 MILLION YEARS AGO

PERMIAN
225 MILLION YEARS TO
279 MILLION YEARS AGO

CARBONIFEROUS
280 MILLION YEARS TO
345 MILLION YEARS AGO

Triceratops

Brachiosaurus

Pteranodon

Corythosaurus

Tyrannosaurus rex

Plesiosaurus

Tylosaurus

Allosaurus

Stegosaurus

Dimorphodon

Camptosaurus

Seismosaurus

Mastodonsaurus

Rutiodon

Protosuchus

Plateosaurus

Eryops

Seymouria

Dimetrodon

Titanophoneus

Urocordylus

Hylonomus

Branchiosaurus